1997

FAMILY VALUES

MARGARET & GERARD O'DONNELL

FAMILY VALUES

The best gift we can give our children

Illustrations by Peter Foster

ST PAULS

FAMILY VALUES: the best gift we can give our children.
© Margaret and Gerard O'Donnell 1993

First published, June 1994

National Library of Australia
Cataloguing-in-Publication data:
O'Donnell, Margaret & Gerard
Family values: the best gift we can give our children
ISBN 1 875570 39 X.
1. Moral education. 2. Children — Conduct of life. 3.Child rearing. I. O'Donnell, Gerard. II. Title.
649.7

Illustrations: Peter Foster
Cover design: Bruno Colombari SSP

Published by
ST PAULS — Society of St Paul
60-70 Broughton Road — (PO Box 230) — Homebush NSW 2140

ST PAULS is an activity of the Priests and Brothers of the Society of St Paul who proclaim the Gospel through the media of social communication.

Contents

Introduction

In January 1989, I travelled with my husband Gerard to Sydney to spend a week attending a workshop run by Professor David Isaacs on the subject of Family Enrichment. Professor Isaacs is Head of the Family Studies Department at the University of Navarre, Pamplona, Spain. He is a tireless exponent of the importance of the family as the basic unit of human society. With eloquence and wit, David Isaacs exposed the relentless attacks of consumerism and political ideologies on the family and the consequences for the fabric of society as a whole.

We were fascinated by Professor Isaacs' ideas on the family and delighted that he had articulated and clarified many of the concerns we had, as parents, in modern society.

Together with a group of friends from Melbourne, we are now completing a course for the Diploma in Family Studies with Professor Isaacs at the University of Navarre. This study has opened up for us a whole new world of understanding of the role and importance of the family in the growth and development of young people, both as children of God and as good citizens, in a world increasingly hostile to the very concept of good and evil.

An important subject in the Family Studies course concerns family values. At the heart of family values is teaching children the human virtues. In this book we will treat the terms 'family values' and 'human virtues' as synonymous. The term *value* is generally used to mean something of great worth whereas *virtue* is somewhat dated and often associated with a reserved or prim and proper manner. Family or human values are those attributes which make us a truly human being of great worth.

As a primary school teacher, I found the course material on the subject of family or human values extremely useful and, by the end of 1991 had prepared a series of class lessons on specific virtues such as generosity and industriousness. The reaction of my Grade 6 children to this teaching was very positive and enthusiastic - evidence of the strength of the family values message rather than the quality of my teaching. These lesson plans and my attempt to explain family values to my class are the foundations upon which this book is built.

It is likely that the lesson plans would have been the only tangible result of our studies with David Isaacs, had it not been for a separate, though closely related, activity we became involved in during 1991. Part of the University of Navarre course requires the students to prepare case studies on various subjects and conduct workshops for parents (mostly enforced recruits among our friends) at which these case studies are presented. In completing this task, our study group aroused the interest of a much larger group of parents in Melbourne. In mid-1991, we agreed to conduct a series of workshops for this group of parents over a period of four evenings. The enthusiasm of these parents for the workshops, particularly the material we presented on family values, finally convinced us to produce this book.

The book is intended for parents who want their children to be happy. Even though parents possess quite natural means for ensuring their children's happiness, nevertheless they should reinforce these means with knowledge and awareness of the family values which we hope this book provides.

The book draws heavily on the work of David Isaacs and in particular his book *Character Building*, for which we wish to express our enormous gratitude.

We have attempted to present our ideas with some humour and by relating anecdotes from real life. We hope that readers draw comfort from the fact that the trials they face in their day-to-day roles as parents are not unique. The anecdotes related in this book are based loosely on our own experience as parents - although our children disclaim any responsibility for the antics of the children mentioned in the stories.

Margaret O'Donnell

1. What are family values?

The best gift we can give our children

Imagine for a moment the young adult, perhaps your own son or daughter, a few years from now.

He or she is sincere, orderly, obedient, industrious, generous, courageous, just, prudent, moderate, patient, persevering, humble, responsible, optimistic and very obviously happy.

Has there ever been such person? Wouldn't you be delighted if your son or daughter was like this person? Isn't this what we all want for our children - not merely for them to grow up to be successful in their careers; not even to be financially secure but to be human beings of great worth and hence know the meaning of true happiness.

The young man or woman described above is a person who has achieved a great deal of human success which, of course, will lead to the achievement of his or her supernatural goal. God made each of us to be as complete a human being as possible. He made us in his own image and likeness. Hence, we all have the potential to be a vision of goodness.

Human values can be acquired by teaching and practice. Just think of how much time we give to our children when we teach them to read, write and count so that they will be fitted to take their places in society. But, often, we do not place enough emphasis on teaching our children human values - to be sincere, generous, industrious or responsible. Yet, the child with these qualities will be much more able to live a full human life than the child who can only read, write and do mathematics adequately.

Most employers demand an interview before offering jobs to prospective employees. The purpose of the interview is usually to gain some insights into the person's character.

A person's character is directly related to their acquisition of human values and not at all related to their academic status.

Our aims for our children must be high - much higher than mere academic success, much greater than financial security. We parents must direct our children to be children of God - children with human values so well developed that they will not only attain happiness for themselves in this life and the next, but will, by their example, lead many others along the path of *Real Happiness*.

If we agree: 'Yes, we do want our children to learn human values', the next question is 'What are human values or virtues?'

When I directed this question recently to a group of 11-year-old children in my class, their answers were diverse, but close to correct in most cases. Values or virtues, they said, are goodness; doing the right thing; things like patience and being generous; loving everyone so you will try to help them; faith, hope, charity; doing something good; being active in doing the right thing; working hard.

Human values - good operative habits

The group of children I questioned earlier clearly associated the word *values* with *goodness*; and even with *operation* or *doing* or *activity*.

But, the *habit* part of values was not at first apparent to them. In order for good actions to be classed as virtues or values, they must be repetitive or regular. A one-off act of charity will not constitute generosity. A person who has the virtue of generosity will, as a matter of habit be generous in his everyday life.

In this book, we are dealing with the *human virtues*. These may also be described as the *natural* or *acquired* virtues.

This makes them different from what many people tend to think of as 'the virtues' - the *Supernatural* or *Infused* virtues, also known as the *theological virtues*.

The theological virtues - faith, hope and charity

The word theological means 'about God'. There are three theological virtues - faith, hope and charity. These theological virtues are infused into a person's soul to enable them to reach their 'supernatural' goal of being with God forever. God freely gives these virtues as gifts and they are directed towards God. These three virtues are first received in the Sacrament of Baptism.

' *Faith is the power to say "Yes" to God by believing what he says to us through his Son and the Church'* (Catechism)

God does not ask us to believe blindly but to endeavour to learn about him and hence to grow in knowledge and love as we become more aware of all he has done for us.

'Hope is the power to trust that God will save us and bring us to heaven through his Son and the Church' (Catechism)

God will never forget us; he has promised to be with us and, if we live as he asks us to, to bring us to heaven for all eternity.

'Charity is the power to love God above all else for his own sake, and our neighbour as ourselves for the love of God' (Catechism)

Parents and teachers should help their children to practise these virtues and make frequent acts of faith, hope, and charity; to ask God to strengthen these virtues within us.

Human values

Human values are different from the supernatural virtues in that they improve a person on the 'natural level'. Human values are not gifts; we acquire them in the same way we acquire an education or physical fitness - through practice and the development of good habits.

Four of these human values are often termed the *cardinal virtues* because all the other natural virtues depend on them. The cardinal virtues are prudence, justice, fortitude and temperance. By grace, these cardinal virtues are made supernatural and serve to orientate a person's human actions to the supernatural final goal.

Prudence and temperance require a degree of reasoning which makes their practice and development more appropriate to an older child or young adult. Fortitude and justice are values more applicable to younger children.

Nevertheless, parents must recognise that prudence and fortitude are necessary in developing any of the other values. Prudence is related to our will and is concerned with choosing good. Prudence keeps our minds focused on why we are practising a certain virtue.

Danger - virtues can become vices!

If we do not exercise prudence, it is likely that a particular virtue will become an end in itself and even a vice. For example, someone may be industrious; but without prudence, this could lead to this 'industry' becoming all important and the person could easily develop a 'workaholic' attitude which would turn the virtue into a vice.

Similarly, whilst orderliness is an excellent virtue, especially for children, we all know that there are people who take orderliness to such an extreme that they can make life unbearable to those around them.

One final example of how each human virtue (except justice) has two vices at the opposite extremes concerns fortitude. We all know people who give up too easily and children especially tend to become discouraged rather quickly. However, a less common but equally destructive vice is shown by the person who refuses to admit defeat even in the face of overwhelming evidence.

Young children don't usually have enough reasoning ability to exercise prudence effectively. This should not stop parents and teachers encouraging them to look carefully and consider situations in which they find themselves. By exercising obedience to their parents, children will gradually learn the range of criteria needed to judge situations. Eventually, they will be in a position to decide for themselves and to choose the good - in other words to exercise prudence.

Parents will also need to exercise the virtue of prudence in order to be clear as to the goals they see for themselves and their children - and to allow for the achievement of these goals within the family situation.

The cardinal virtue of prudence will need to be developed in relation to other human values and, to some degree, will need to be considered by parents in the teaching of each value at each age level.

2. Why teach human values?

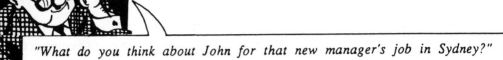

"What do you think about John for that new manager's job in Sydney?"

"John? You mean that young man in Engineering whose only been with us for a couple of years".

"Yes, that's him. What do you think of him?"

"Well, I hadn't thought of him for the job but now that you mention it, I must say he is impressive"

"In what way?"

"Well, he's a hard worker for a start - very diligent and sticks at the job till it finished. And he's honest - you can't trust half of those people in Engineering but with John you know he means exactly what he says. Yes, and I've noticed that he's always ready to help out the other Engineers when there's a problem and always so cheerful about it. Something else which is becoming more important these days with all this talk of sexual harassment around, I've noticed John is not one those who stand around the coffee machine telling dirty jokes and leering at the women in the office. Yes, now that you mention it, John would be ideal for that job in Sydney".

"You're right, John does have a lot of the human virtues".

"Virtues. What do you mean - virtues? No, no, I don't think he's one of those religious types - he's just a really decent person - nothing to do with virtues!"

Teaching young people family or human values may seem to some people rather strange in this day and age. This may have something to do with modern popular culture which seems to glorify the anti-hero - the rebel - the person who rejects conventional ideas of good and evil. Values are not seen as being much help to a person wanting to make his way in a 'selfish world'.

There are also many people who would say 'We don't want to brainwash our children; let them make up their own minds as to what is good and what is bad'. Others may think that children cannot improve the way they behave and that the children will simply pick up their parents' own good and bad habits 'Oh, our Johnny's very messy - but you can't blame him, his father is just the same!'

Some may believe that all this talk of values is just common sense and no great effort is needed on the part of parents to develop good habits in their children - somehow this will all happen automatically.

Parents - the best teachers of family values

Parents are the primary educators of their children. Parents work, together with God, to give life to their child and in so doing, must accept responsibility for the child. It is the parents' duty, as well as their right, to take responsibility for the spiritual and material welfare of the child. This does not mean that they need to tackle this important task alone. Parents should look for and utilise any person or means at their disposal to aid them in this privileged work. However, they should never delegate absolute responsibility to anyone.

School teachers, clergy and friends will all be needed for advice, direction and help but the parent is the primary educator of the child.

The family - school of the human values

God instituted the family. The family is the only natural organisation. A child is born into this organisation because God with his infinite knowledge and wisdom sees that, in this environment, the child is able to reach full potential - to be the person that God wants him/her to be.

Schools are human organisations; most of them very useful and necessary, and many doing great work to supplement the education of the child. The school does not, and can never, take the place of the family. In the family, the child is loved from the moment he/she is born - loved for what he/she is not for what he/she does. In any other human organisation, the child is appreciated only for what he/she does. In school, he/she studies mathematics, language and a host of other subjects, but it is not acceptable for him/her to be in school and not be learning. The school's purpose is to be there to give the child the opportunity to learn and acquire knowledge and skills in a variety of areas.

> *But the family is there for the child to live, to grow, to be. The home should be the first, and most important, school of human values.*

This isn't to say that schools should not teach human values. Children should continue to develop this learning at school. Structured lessons should be given to help children to gain knowledge of human values and encourage them to practise these values. Nevertheless, it is still undeniable that the parents, in the context of the family unit, are the best educators of human values. Most of the child's early years are spent in and around the home with their parents. This gives parents the unique opportunity to ensure that values are practised regularly, that advantage is taken of naturally arising opportunities for teaching values and that time can be given to talk to each child individually about his or her acquisition of particular values.

Parents - true professionals

Parents should never feel inadequate in teaching values. God did not judge them inadequate to share in giving life to the child. By the very nature of their being parents, they have been given, by God, the task of educating their children in the human values and God will give them the grace to carry out this obligation.

Time is often at a premium. Some parents may consider there is not enough time to teach children family values. Priority is an important consideration here. So too is professionalism. In any occupation, we try to be as professional as possible, whether we are office workers, doctors or teachers. Being professional means that we make sure we have full knowledge of what we need to do and we do it to the best of our ability, taking into account those factors which are relevant to the occupation.

So too, we must be professional in our role as parents. Being a parent is not something we do in the time we have left over from our 'proper' jobs. It should be the most important role in our lives.

To bring up our children to be wonderful human beings who will be really happy here on earth and, ultimately, happy forever in Heaven and by their example, show others how to live as children of God. There is no greater profession than this privileged task entrusted to us by God - that of being **The professional parent**.

3. How do we teach human values?

*If a person would set to work to cultivate one new virtue and weed
out one old vice every year, he would soon become a saint.*

Thomas A'Kempis

In order to teach human values to our children, we parents need to be true professionals. This implies that we make every effort to ensure we are equipped for the task. As parents, there are four areas we need to consider in thinking about how to teach human values:

1. We need a sound knowledge of the values.

2. We need to set a good example in the practice of human values.

3. We must be aware of the opportunities for teaching human values (what we might call the methodology).

4. We must be demanding in regard to the practice of human values in ourselves and our children.

A sound knowledge of the values

As parents, we need to be clear in our own minds what each of the particular human values entails. This book outlines five values or virtues most appropriate to children prior to adolescence. It describes in some detail what constitutes each of these values and how we, as parents, might teach these values to our children.

For further detail on these values and others, David Isaacs' book *Character Building* is highly recommended as a most informative text. In general terms, parents need to be clear in their knowledge of what constitutes a virtue or value.

How effectively children acquire a value is determined by the intensity with which it is practised and the motive which lies behind its practice. For example, let us consider the virtue of industriousness. If we are industrious only when the work appeals to us, or when we are feeling fit and fresh, then the intensity of practice is not very strong. Development is not really possible unless we can apply ourselves industriously even to tasks we dislike or when we are tired.

As parents we must also be aware of the importance of motivation in respect to practising values. Children who study hard to pass a test because they have been promised a new bike as a reward are motivated quite differently from the children who study hard because their parents and teachers expect them to do the best they can. I leave it to you to choose which of these children has the better motivation to acquire the value of industriousness.

Parents will often be responsible themselves for motivating the child in the practice of a value. Ideas for motivating children are given in this book in the Chapter devoted to each specific value.

Set a good example

Fortunately for the human race, parents do not need to be perfect themselves in a particular value in order to teach it well. In fact, we will often be a better example for the child if we ourselves are striving to improve in relation to that value.

A mother of four was finding orderliness a difficult value to practise herself, but she accepted that her children were learning more from seeing her efforts than they would if she was constantly reminding them to be orderly. When she organised the kitchen cupboards so that everyone knew where things should be kept, she found that some of the children followed her example and began organising their own rooms in a more orderly fashion.

Perfection in a particular value may, in fact, make it more difficult for a parent to teach it. Whereas, if we, as parents, need to make an effort, we are more likely to be aware of the effort the child is making and we can modify our demands and praise accordingly.

Whether we like it or not, we will be an example to our children and we will teach them by this example. It remains for us to decide if this example will be good or bad - will we teach them to be virtuous or educate our children in vices?

If we never give donations to charities or missions, yet spend a great deal of money on ourselves, we should not be surprised if our children turn out to be mean and inconsiderate and totally lacking in generosity.

Habits will be formed in children and to a large degree be dependent on the example of parents. It is vital that this example is good example and leads to the development of human values.

Be aware of opportunities for teaching human values

One of the chief aims of this book is to help parents to develop and extend their awareness of the opportunities for teaching human values to their children. In each chapter, we will look at a specific value and point out a few ways in which parents can teach this value to their children.

These examples are not meant to be prescriptive but, rather, starting points. Some parents may use the actual examples as suggested; others may use them as a starting point to lead to the awareness of other ways, more relevant to their situation, in which they can develop the value in their children.

The methodology for parents to use in teaching values to their children is described in each chapter under three headings:

1. Talking with the Child

2. Using everyday events of family life

3. Structuring events or activities (formal or informal planning)

Some parents may find that using naturally-occurring events is the most practical and efficient way of teaching values to their children. Some parents may decide it is the only method they wish to use. Others may prefer the structured activities - either the actual ones given, or activities which they have deliberately structured to be appropriate to the value development and relevant to their particular child.

Talking with the child may be a favoured method in some instances and with some children.

A combination of all three methods may be relevant to families where the children differ in temperament.

As parents, our experience has been that we use a combination of the three methods. Naturally-occurring family situations usually require less effort on the part of the parents, as long as we are aware and always on the look out for an opportunity to use them.

Structured activities can be very effective with some children but less so with others.

Talking to the child, we find rewarding from a motivational point of view but it is usually necessary to combine talking, with one of the other two methods to incorporate it as part of the practice of the value.

How parents choose to use this book will depend upon the particular needs of their children and their family.

Be demanding

This is positive advice. Many people equate being demanding with taking away the children's freedom. Freedom is a word greatly misused by society in general and by adolescents in particular. It is quite common nowadays to hear young people say 'I don't want to do this or that, I want my freedom'. However, freedom exists only if a person is able to make a choice. A person who cannot read has no choice whether or not to read poetry or non-fiction. That person is deprived of freedom because of the inability to read. The person who can read is free to choose which book to read even whether to read or not.

Hence, by helping our children to acquire human values, we are helping them to be free. They will be free to be generous or not, as they wish. However, if generosity has no real meaning for them, they will be unable to choose - in other words they will be deprived of their freedom of choice.

In order for children to acquire the human values, we must make demands on them that lead them to an active practice of the virtues. We need to be constantly requiring them to engage in repetitive acts of generosity, industriousness or patience in order to enable them to develop these good operative habits.

Parents must at all times see their role as educators of their children in a positive light. In respect to human values, they should try to get to know their children, to find out which of the values they are fairly well equipped with and into which they need to put the most attention. Parents will automatically practise industriousness, patience, fortitude, perseverance, responsibility and optimism in their endeavours to educate their children in human values.

We began this chapter with the statement that parents need to be professional in their role of teaching values to their children. It is not an easy role but it can be achieved with awareness, effort, dedication and the help of God's grace.

4. When do we teach which values?

My practice is to write out a list of thirteen virtues from Temperance and Order, to Sincerity and Humility, then concentrate on each in turn for only one week, then start with number one again, so that I could go through the complete course in thirteen weeks, and four courses in a year.

Benjamin Franklin

When do we teach which values? The short answer to this question is 'as early as possible'. We do suggest that even the little toddler can and should be expected to learn about, and practise some human values. There are three main factors we need to think about when considering when to teach which value - the actual value itself, the particular features of the age levels and the specific needs of the child, parent and family.

Some values are more suited to particular age levels

Orderliness can be taught to a very small child and be practised by the child as he/she develops the habit of tidying away his/her toys.

On the other hand, the virtue of loyalty needs a well developed intellect in order to understand the very nature of the virtue. It would not be possible to teach this value with any real understanding to a six-year-old. This value is much better tackled around the age of sixteen when the child's reasoning is more fully developed.

Each age level has its own particular features

Each age level has well recognised features which make one value more relevant than another. The eight-year-old is beginning to focus for the first time on people and events outside the home. Therefore, this is a good age to consider teaching those values concerned with others such as responsibility and generosity. The twelve-year-old may need to be taught about modesty.

Don't forget - children, parents and family may have specific needs

Each family should consider this matter for themselves in deciding which value they will teach and when. The personality of the child is a major consideration. The four- year-old child, who finds it hard to be generous, may need help to practise generosity even at a very early age. On the other hand a nine-year-old sister, who is naturally generous, may not need specific help until she is older and able to appreciate that being generous also means being generous with her time.

Parents must also consider their own specific needs. Some parents may consider industriousness important even for a six-year-old. Others may believe that this value is not important until the age of, say, eleven years.

The various situations in which the family finds itself may dictate the selection of values and the timing of their teaching. The family may be in a special situation at some point in time which directs the parents to teach a particular value regardless of the ages of the children.

Family values to the rescue at a time of family trauma

I remember a few years ago when Dad had to go overseas at a most inappropriate time for the family. David was fourteen and at that very 'difficult' early adolescent age. Louise was school-age and Clare was still a very young child. The family was finding it tough just to cope with this situation when Dad had to go overseas for two months on assignment. Clearly, the only way Mum would survive was if the two older children took on a great deal of extra responsibility. Both David and Louise were given well structured instructions on the additional tasks they would have to carry out and both were told that the next two months would be a time when they were to be very 'responsible'. In normal circumstances, we would never have dreamt of giving the children such an intense period of practice in the virtue of responsibility. But the family's needs dictated this course of action and we are delighted to report that the family survived the ordeal and David, in particular, was a paragon of responsibility during those months.

Which value to teach and when, depends on the nature of the value, the characteristics of the age level and is often dictated by the needs of the child, the parents and the family itself. Being aware of these factors, parents should adopt their own timing and selection of which values to teach.

To assist in this process, the following is a guide to the teaching of values at a time appropriate to the nature of the value and the age level of the child. This guide is derived from the work of David Isaacs in his book *Character Building*.

The childhood phase (0-7 years)

The childhood phase lasts from birth to the age of about seven and is normally seen as comprising two separate stages - infancy (0-3 years) and pre-school/early school (3-7 years).

Infancy (0-3 years)

Infancy is the most dynamic period of the child's life. Children learn very fast in the first three years and learn from copying the examples of those around them - especially their mother's. They master the gross motor skills of walking and running, talk proficiently and are able to understand much of what is going on in the day-to-day life of the family.

Pre-school/early school (3-7years)

During this stage, the children enter a period of development which is characterised by a first awakening of themselves as individuals. Dad becomes an important part of their life and the child gradually moves to discover the world outside of the home.

At this age, the child can understand rules but has little reasoning ability. Neither is this a particularly social age - the child's attention remains within the home situation.

Values for early childhood

Given these characteristics, parents should seek to teach the human values of obedience, sincerity, orderliness and generosity to children of this age. These values are closely related to the efficient functioning of the family and the place and contribution of the young child to the family.

Because young children have poorly developed reasoning powers, obedience should be taught as early as possible. Bearing in mind the tender age of the children, parents must make only reasonable demands on them. These demands must be clear to the children and within their range of understanding. Children must be encouraged to obey 'to be loving and helpful for Mum and Dad'. This motive is infinitely better than demanding obedience 'for fear of punishment'.

A similar motivation is needed to guide a child to be generous. Young children tend to sway from one extreme to the other where generosity is concerned. It is not unusual for very young children to refuse to share any of their possessions with others. The 'Terrible-Twos' phase of childhood development is frequently punctuated by screams from children if another child tries to play with their toys. This is quite natural.

> ### 'That's our David - not yours!'
>
> *Once when Clare was two years old, we were watching her older brother, David, competing at a country swim meet. One of the other parents from our swimming club started to shout 'Go, David' only to be told off by an indignant Clare - 'That's our David, not yours. Don't shout for him!'*

Nevertheless, parents need to have control of the situation. Because of the tendency of young children not to be generous, this is a good time to begin teaching of generosity.

Another human value which can be taught at this age is sincerity. Young children find it easy to be sincere. They have a small circle of people to whom they relate - usually only Mum and Dad, so the possibility for them to disclose feelings to others is not available to them.

Young children will make full disclosure because this comes naturally to them and because they are untrained in withholding information. They also have no need to do so. This initial disclosure will involve more and more thought as children mature and so the virtue of sincerity will develop as children learn to think about what they will disclose and to whom. Development of other human values including generosity and obedience will require the child to think and act sincerely. This make the virtue of sincerity a pre-requisite for learning other values.

Another value, we recommend at this stage is that of orderliness. It is so much easier for children to acquire this good habit at an early age rather than later. Once acquired, orderliness will lead to the development of other values, particularly industriousness. Orderliness is also a priority value for family peace and calm. Orderly parents and children are more in control of their family life than disorderly ones.

Childhood maturity - the golden age of childhood (8-12 years)

This stage is often called the Golden Age because the difficult early, teething years are behind the children and they have not reached the even more difficult adolescent growing years. It is a settled phase for most children. The children start to focus on events and people outside the home, find everything interesting - and are very interesting themselves.

Values for childhood maturity

Children become more social during this phase and so development of the human value of responsibility is appropriate at this age since it is directly concerned with others.

Another characteristic of this stage of growth is that children now start to direct their attention to what they are doing. So the values of fortitude, perseverance, patience and industriousness are important in leading them to focus on the use of the will. Strengthening the will is important now before children reach the turbulent years of adolescence when will-power is an important factor in young people's maturity, as they are called upon to make their own life commitments.

Puberty and early adolescence (13-15 years)

At this age, children are generally engaged in major psychological, emotional and physical changes. They become critical of themselves and others - more often than not their parents - as they struggle with an awakening of their own identity. They seek to find out who they are and what their role in life is. In this search, they relate more easily to people of their own age and are generally more susceptible to influences outside the home - regardless of whether these influences are good or bad.

At this age, children are looking for reasons, and the best way for parents to relate to children in these difficult years is to give them reasons. This does not mean that we should sit for hours reasoning with the child. In fact that is more likely to do more harm than good. The reasons should be given, but given, as David Isaacs would say, according to the three "C's" - *clearly, concisely* and then, *change* the subject.

Do not despair - the child will listen to reason although this may not occur until the final phase of childhood - true adolescence.

Values for early adolescence

In light of these characteristics of early adolescence, it is advisable to emphasise the human values of modesty and moderation - both of which have as their cardinal virtue that of temperance. Development of these values will help young adolescents control their passions.

Also important at this stage are the values of sociability, friendship and respect - all of which are related to the young adolescents' relationships with others. Good development of these values will ensure that the bad influences of society don't harm children as they search for their place in relationship to others.

True adolescence (16-18 years)

By now, young people have an increased ability to reason things out and will listen to reason. This is the time to emphasise values which require a highly developed reasoning power.

Values for true adolescence

The cardinal virtue of prudence leads the way in the values to be emphasised at this age, closely followed by flexibility, understanding, humility, loyalty and optimism - all of which cannot be covered in any depth before this stage of development.

Above all else - optimism

Many of us will be parents ourselves before we appreciate these virtues fully but that should not stop us teaching children to be humble and optimistic at an early age.

Optimism is probably the most contagious of all human values. We firmly believe that optimistic parents will not only help their own children to be optimistic but also all those with whom they come into contact. How often have you heard it said 'It feels good just to be in her company'. What they often mean is 'When I'm with an optimistic person, I feel optimistic myself'. Unfortunately, the reverse applies - but pessimists don't have too many friends to influence.

In this book we will concentrate on primary school-aged children, the child prior to adolescence - up to the age of twelve years. Consequently, we will detail only those values which we see as applying to these younger children.

We must stress that the stages of development described above are for guidance only. Some children are very sociable at four and reasoning well by the age of eleven. Others will still be in the golden age of childhood at fourteen. Similarly the lists of values applicable to each stage of development is also for guidance only. It is not meant to be prescriptive.

Family life is spontaneous, full of love and joy. Families comprise individuals with different needs, different strengths and weaknesses and different abilities. Parents are offered this guide to the teaching of human values with this in mind. Take it and use it as you will. If you are reading this book, you are already well aware of the importance of teaching values to your children.

> *Awareness is the first and possibly the most important attribute you will need.*

Meet the values family

Hello, my name is Mark. I'm only ten months old and people think I don't know very much - just because I can't talk yet.

They don't realise just how much I notice about the things that go on around my family. If you like, I will explain to you what the older people in my family are really saying and just how good they are at these things they call *VALUES*.

First of all let me introduce the rest of my family.

This is my sister Clare -
She's seven years old.

And this is my other sister Louise -
She's twelve years old.

David is my **big** brother -
He's eighteen years old.

And this is my
Mum and Dad -
I'm not sure but I think
they're **very** old!

Smart Mark talks about obedience

HERE'S ANOTHER OF HER FAVOURITE *TRICKS!*

CLARE, WILL YOU TAKE THIS CARROT AND FEED THE RABBIT, PLEASE.

JUST A MINUTE, MUM! I'M IN THE BATHROOM!

I KNOW WHAT SHE'S UP TO! SHE'S DECIDED TO DODGE THIS JOB BY STAYING OUT OF THE WAY FOR FIVE MINUTES. BY *THEN*, MUM WILL HAVE DONE IT, HERSELF!

I DON'T THINK THAT WAS VERY OBEDIENT, DO YOU?

WHERE ON EARTH IS CLARE? OH, I SUPPOSE I'LL HAVE TO FEED THE RABBIT *MYSELF*, OR THE POOR THING WILL STARVE!

TEE HEE!

— 36 —

5. Obedience

Children, even very young children, are quite good at avoiding obedience. They do, however, become even better at this as they get older. If you think seven-year-old Clare is good at avoiding obedience, you should see her twelve-year-old sister - her excuses are masterpieces.

So what is involved in the human value of obedience, and how do parents tackle the problems of disobedience and encourage children to obey?

There are three aspects of obedience that parents must look at if children are to develop this very important habit. Children must:

1. *recognise and accept the parents' authority;*

2. *convert the parents' request into their own decison - this involves an act of the will;*

3. *carry out, promptly, what has been requested and try to do it as the parents meant it to be done.*

Recognising and accepting authority

Young children intuitively recognise the authority of their parents. Parents provide for all their needs and children rely on their parents. Naturally, they automatically accept their parents' authority.

As children get older, they need to be guided to appreciate the authority of other people - teachers, the police, sports coaches, in fact anyone in whose care they are placed.

This means that parents themselves must give a good example of obedience to their children. Children who see that Dad will exceed the speed limit whenever he sees there are no police patrols around, are receiving a clear message that Dad has no regard for the rules of the road and does not accept the authority of those who made them.

It is a short step from this lesson for children to conclude that obedience is only something that has to be done if you can't get away with disobedience.

Converting another's request into one's own decision

Young children obey out of love and affection for their parents or because they unconsciously recognise that their parents' requests are best for them. Obedience, then, is closely related to prudence in very young children - the five-year-olds who obey their parents are exercising prudence as far as they are able.

From about the age of five, children need to be given reasons for obedience so that they will eventually be able to take the demand from their parents and convert it into their own decision.

Parents will find countless opportunities during the day to make requests of their children and require their obedience - and provide perfectly practical reasons why the children should obey. Ask them to pour drinks for dinner - why - because if you don't, you will go thirsty!

As children reach the later stages of childhood maturity, the best reason for obedience is simple - it is God's will that they obey the fourth commandment.

Promptly carry out the request and do it as the person in authority meant it to be done

The problems encountered earlier, in asking Clare to be obedient, can be avoided if there is an awareness at all times of how skillful children may be at avoiding obeying orders. This means being very observant and sensitive to the reactions of children.

Demands must be few, clear, and made in an affectionate way - then followed up to make sure they are obeyed. Even when making requests of toddlers as young as two years old, parents must make sure that they comply with the request - and praise them warmly when they do. Most young children want to be 'good' - so you cannot say often enough 'good girl/boy' when the toddler completes even a simple request like 'bring me that toy'.

This means that parents must be consistent in the matter of obedience - for most of us this is easy, *every single request* from the parents must be carried out unless extenuating circumstances prevent the child from so doing.

By following up the demands made on Clare, Mum would have realised that Clare did not clear up the toys as she had intended. Being aware of the excuses and the myriad of ways of avoiding obedience which children dream up, Mum would have made a point of not feeding the rabbit when Clare dodged into the bathroom. She would have waited for Clare and insisted that she did the job even if this caused inconvenience for Mum at a later stage.

Of course, sometimes there may be a very good reason why a child suggests waiting rather than obeying immediately. Imagine that Mum had asked Clare to find a clean nappy for Mark. Clare may have replied 'Don't change him now, Mum, we're going to the shops soon and he'll need another change before we go.' This may be an excuse to avoid obedience or it may be a genuine suggestion to save time. If so, Mum should be sensitive to, and recognise this, as an opportunity for both praise and teaching another virtue - responsibility.

Parents who are observant, sensitive and aware will be able to judge these situations for themselves.

How do we teach our children to obey

Talking with the child

Inspiration from scripture and the saints

The parable of the two sons is a good scriptural reference to use as a discussion point on obedience with young children. (Mt 21: 28-32). This example relates how the father told his two sons that he wanted them to work in the vineyard. The elder son said 'No' but thought better of this reaction and went to work as his father had asked him to. The younger son said 'Yes' but then did not go. Obviously, doing is the essence of obedience and not the words we say.

St Joseph acted obediently to every request made of him. He took Mary as his wife when told to by the angel and obediently followed instructions to flee to Egypt in the middle of the night with Mary and Jesus.

Jesus, we are told, went with his parents to Nazareth and lived in obedience to them until he began his public ministry at the age of 30 years (Lk 2: 51).

Many great saints provide inspirational examples of obedience. St Catherine Labouré spent 46 years of her life obediently performing menial tasks for the sick and aged in a hospice in Paris. She had been the recipient of visions of Our Lady and yet continued to work obediently and humbly on whatever tasks she was given.

St Aloysius Gonzaga, although a young, outstanding student of philosophy and theology, obediently accepted the task of teaching catechism to young children and caring for the sick - doing this work with generous dedication.

Religious orders have as one of their three vows, the vow of obedience, suggesting its importance to those who wish to dedicate their lives to God.

Everyday activities we can use to teach obedience

There are many instances within a normal day which can be used to help children to practise obedience. In fact, the problem with obedience is not having to invent situations for its practice but rather to limit the number of situations which arise quite naturally.

Too much - Too hard - Too boring

If seven-year-olds are given ten instructions in half an hour, they will find it virtually impossible to cope. At best, they will decide for themselves to do some of them and leave the rest. Worse still, they might mindlessly carry out all the tasks just to get them out of the way. Either way, they are not practising obedience.

Remember that they need to consider the request of another and make it their own decision. For this process to work, parents must not make too many demands on children - especially trivial demands. Rather, they should consciously pay attention to only a few situations in the day when they will require children to be obedient.

Consistency

Suppose, on Saturday, Mum makes a big fuss that Clare must wear her old shoes when she is playing in the garden. On Sunday, Clare again wants to play in the garden but Mum has just cleaned her old shoes, so she allows Clare to go out in her new shoes. Through this inconsistency, Mum is suggesting to Clare that there was no real reason for her obedience on Saturday - this will hinder Clare's development of the virtue of obedience.

Clarity

Clarity of information is essential if children are to develop obedience. For very young children, the information must be simple and short. And with very young children the reason for the request must also be simple - 'Because I asked you to' - especially if the reasoning is complicated. However, if possible it is always best to give children a clear reason for the things that you ask them to do.

Certainly, older children need reasons. Requests made of older children should be thought out carefully by parents. For example, we are going on a family outing and could say to eighteen-year-old David:

'We want you to come to Aunt Peggy's on Sunday and make sure you wear a clean white shirt, tie and your best pants and shoes'.

In fact, how David is dressed is trivial compared with the fact that he comes with the family on this visit - so we limit our request accordingly:

'We are going to visit Aunt Peggy on Sunday and we would like you to come with us because this is family occasion'.

This example is, of course, a matter of personal choice and parents need to make their own decisions about what is important and what is trivial. Then, having made the decision, they must spell these out clearly to the child.

Prompt obedience

As long as the parents have carefully considered the request, it should be carried out promptly. If we know that Louise is watching the end of her favourite show on television, we may decide to wait and ask her to take the rubbish out when it is finished.

If, on the other hand, she has been glued to the television for the last two hours and, when asked to remove the rubbish, says she will do it when the program is finished, she is making a poor response to obedience. She needs to learn that jobs should be done as soon as the request is made.

In a similar vein, regularly giving children tasks to be done later is not a good idea since it builds in the child the habit of delay - one of the preliminary habits on the way to regular disobedience.

Constant vigilance is required if parents are to avoid the familiar excuse for disobedience - 'Of course, I'll do it - later'. Especially with older children, parents should generally insist that a job is done now as long as the requests are few, reasonable, and sensitive to the situation.

In every family, there comes that one time in the day when the virtue of obedience is tested - bedtime. It is at bedtime that the full power of the imagination of disobedient children comes into play. Parents need to be clear about what time bedtime is, consistent in applying bedtime rules, give reasons for particular bedtimes on particular nights - perhaps early bedtime on Sundays because of school the next day - and especially vigilant about the delaying tactics - 'Oh, but I haven't had my supper yet'.

Structured examples of obedience

Rules of the road

With young children, these may be simple rules of stop, look, listen. With older children more complex cycling rules may be presented to be obeyed.

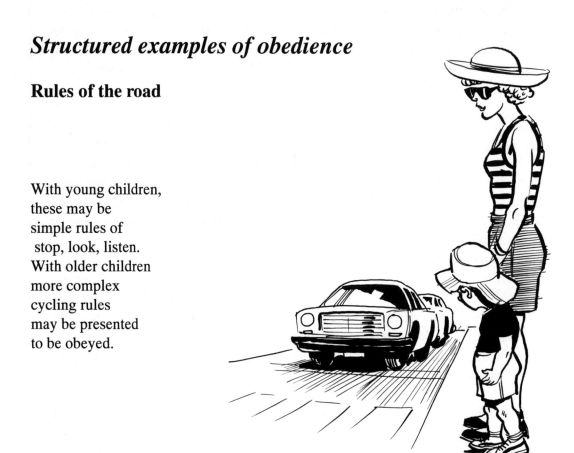

Stop - look - listen Children as young as two-three years can learn to stop at the kerb, look both ways, listen for cars and, if the road is clear, walk straight across. The process of obeying these instructions is for very good reasons. Children may be killed by a fast car. The rules are there to keep us safe. The rules are given clearly and carefully to children and repeated often. There is consistency - every time children reach a kerb, the parent says 'Stop, look, listen'. When the road is clear, they walk straight across, looking and listening, not chatting or dawdling but concentrating on obeying the rules of the road made to protect us all.

Make up a cardboard road for young children and get them to teach their play people the rules of the road.

Obeying the rules of the sporting club, music, scout or guide group

Older children can learn much by being members of sporting groups or being involved with other cultural disciplines, such as Scouts, Guides or Orchestral groups, which involve obeying rules.

In order to operate efficiently, each group has certain rules. Children learn that the rules are there for a reason and that they help themselves and the group by practising the virtue of obedience.

The Swimming Club

Louise belongs to the local swimming club. As a member of the Junior A Team, she is expected to train on certain nights of the week, be available for competitions and wear the Club uniform. Obviously, she can neglect one or more of these rules and still be a member of the Club but she knows that to be a true member, she must obey the Club rules. Even half hearted commitment to some of the rules will reduce the benefit to herself and other members of the team.

The School Orchestra

So too with other groups. Children who are members of the school orchestra will let the whole orchestra down if they do not practise the particular piece for next month's concert. Even if they practise their work, play beautifully on the night, but refuse to wear the orchestral uniform, they will again be a hindrance to the group.

Most children who belong to such groups can see the need for obedience to the rules - often they are more pedantic about these rules than their parents - having to be at the swimming pool for training at exactly five o'clock - not one minute to or one minute after, exactly five o'clock. All this means is that the parents have a great opportunity to teach obedience in these situations.

Parents will have many opportunities to encourage obedience in their children. Obedience will become a virtue in children as they learn to recognise and accept authority, convert these demands into their own decisions and carry out these demands promptly and cheerfully.

Smart Mark talks about sincerity

6. Sincerity

Of all the human values, sincerity is the one we seem to forget as we become older. Parents are often guilty, as Smart Mark notices, of giving their children bad examples of sincerity. As children, we don't know how to be insincere but as we grow up, how often during the day do we fail in sincerity. In fact, sincerity in an adult is often regarded as naivety. Yet, we know in our hearts that sincerity is the most important inter-personal virtue.

How often do we write 'Yours sincerely' in closing a letter? Do we really mean we are 'sincere'? What is sincerity and what does it involve?

Sincerity involves us revealing totally, thoughts, deeds, feelings or experiences. However, there are three very important factors which determine these revelations.

To be sincere, these total revelations must be:

1. appropriate

2. to the right person

3. at the right time

It would be totally inappropriate for young children to tell their teacher or school friends that their mothers do not like Mrs. Jones because she talks too much. This revelation is unnecessary and totally inappropriate (not to mention embarrassing).

If the revelation is appropriate, it is vital that it is directed to the right person in order for this to constitute sincerity. Children who have a problem with school work certainly need to tell someone about this situation. But there is no sincerity involved in revealing this to a school friend. This revelation needs to be made to parents or teachers or someone who is really in a position to do something about it.

The third factor of importance in ensuring sincerity in revealing thoughts, words, deeds or feelings is that it must be at the right time. For example, a young boy tells his father that his brother was using the garage tools three weeks ago without permission. This revelation is not sincere because it is not made at the right time. It is appropriate, it is to the right person but three weeks after the incident is not the right time.

'If we could see ourselves as others see us'

When the Scottish poet, Robbie Burns, wrote these famous words, he was not attempting to educate his readers in sincerity. But each of us does need to be able to see ourselves, not necessarily as others see us but as we really are. To be sincere with others, we need to begin by being sincere with ourselves.

But who really knows you? Do you know yourself better than anyone else knows you? Does Mum really know her child? Does a young boy really know his father or his brother?

Is it easier to know a two-year-old child or a twelve-year-old child? Obviously the two year-old child is quite open, hides nothing, what you see is what you get. On the other hand, a twelve-year-old could easily have learned to deceive and hide things.

Little children are sincere because they have not learnt how to deceive and hide. Jesus told us that we must be sincere like little children in order to enter the kingdom of heaven. The very small child epitomises sincerity.

Seeing things as they really are

Children need to distinguish between:

1. what is important and what is not important
2. what is fact and what is fiction
3. what is fact and what is opinion (older children).

Parents play a vital role in encouraging their children to be sincere. They need to be clear about what is really important and what is unimportant or of lesser importance.

Take, for example, the situation where children are not hungry enough to eat all their sandwich at lunch time. So they hide the remaining portion in their school bag. The parent's reaction to this deception is vital if sincerity is to be encouraged.

In one scenario, the parent could insist that the children eat the squashed remains of the sandwich as a punishment for wasting good food. This would achieve little, except perhaps to encourage them to find a better hiding place next time they want to discard their lunch.

An alternative approach could be for the parent to explain to the children that if they cannot eat all their food, it needs to be carefully wrapped up and brought home so that someone else can eat it later. There is no need for children to be deceptive -it is all right for them to leave what they do not want. They are encouraged to reveal their feelings to the right person - their parent.

Of course, this example is not about wasting food but about encouraging children to be open about their likes and dislikes and subsequently about other feelings.

Differentiating between fact and fiction

Once again, the parents need to be perceptive, vigilant and aware of how to encourage the human value of sincerity. It is not uncommon for younger children to have pretend friends or to pretend that their teddy bears speak to them. These fictional characters and happenings are very healthy signs of a vivid imagination which children quickly grow out of.

A parent who scolds children in this situation, perhaps even calling it lying, will make the practice of sincerity very difficult for children . The most likely result will be that children continue to talk to the teddy bear or pretend friend but stop telling their parents about it. This could be the start of a lengthy practice at insincerity on the part of children.

The parent who understands that children may use a pretend friend if they are unsure of something or maybe even for fun, can gradually and sensitively replace the fictional character with a toy or a pet or even themselves. If children feel free to talk about the fictional character and the fictional things that character says, they can be brought to see it as such. On the other hand, if the parents do not allow children to discuss the fiction how can they know how the children really feel?

'Big Ted did it!'

One method of teaching sincerity which we find useful with our children between the ages of about four-seven years started when our eldest son, David, was about that age. It is now a standard family joke. David had a large teddy bear which we named, not surprisingly 'Big Ted'. One day when David was four years old, he had made rather a mess of his bedroom and Mum demanded angrily 'David, who made this mess in your bedroom?' 'Oh, it must have been Big Ted, I suppose', said David innocently. Needless to say, Mum was unable to stay angry for long after that piece of quick thinking. So she said 'Well you and Big Ted had better clean up the mess before you come down for supper!'

After that, any time that Big Ted got the blame for things that went wrong, we knew that David had been up to mischief. Later, it became a way for David to more easily own up to things he had done wrong. By the age of about seven years David had got into the habit of practising sincerity in matters such as these.

Big Ted has been handed down to all our other children and continues to be used as a useful 'scapegoat' for a few years while the child learns the virtue of sincerity. So, when we hear that 'Big Ted did it' we know that an opportunity to teach sincerity has just presented itself.

Differentiating between fact and opinion

This is a difficult area even for many adults. Parents and teachers have the duty to use the words *fact* and *opinion* often with their children so that the difference becomes easy to spot.

Surprising though it may seem, the difficulty parents face in helping their children to distinguish between fact and opinion is **not** that a whole lot of conflicting and erroneous ideas are presented as fact. If they were it would be easy for parents to logically refute the erroneous points put forward. Unfortunately, the opposite is the case. Most ideas seen on television or read in the press are put forward as opinions and time and time again the message is that there are **no such things as facts - only opinions.**

But let us examine a more straightforward case of fact and opinion. When two different stories emerge following a dispute between two children (who started the fight?), one of the most important ways to solve the dispute is for the adult to clarify the facts. This needs to be done clearly and concisely. As parents, we need to be wary of expressions such as 'I think ...', 'He was going to...' and 'I thought that...', and to concentrate on the bare facts.

Practice will improve the discerning of fact from opinion but it is often a difficult area especially when dealing with children who have a problem with sincerity. Perhaps it is these children who grow up to be journalists and politicians and present their opinions as though they were facts!

We all need to be able to read between the lines and identify the facts.

A word of caution

Adults do not always find sincerity an easy virtue to practise. Young children will tell you if they think your hair or dress is awful. Adults will often flatter you regardless of what they think. This is because they have learned that sincerity must always be governed by prudence and charity.

St Augustine wrote:

> *Although everyone who lies is attempting to conceal the truth,*
> *not everyone who conceals the truth is actually lying.*

In order to practise sincerity, we must be aware that the truth should be disclosed clearly. We must have confidence in the person to whom we are making the revelation - they are there to help, not to judge us. Our explanation must be courageous, clear and as unemotional as possible.

Practising sincerity will help us to see ourselves and others clearly and so help us to improve and become the person God wants us to be.

How do we teach our children to be sincere?

Talking with the child

Inspiration from scripture and the saints

Jesus told us, during his time on earth, that we should all be like little children.

On one occasion, Jesus was asked 'Who is the greatest in the Kingdom of Heaven?' He replied by calling over a young child and warning the people that, unless they became like little children, they would not enter the kingdom of heaven. (Mt 18 : 1-5).

On another occasion, when the disciples of Jesus were trying to move children away from him, Jesus said 'Let the children come to me and do not stop them because the kingdom of heaven belongs to such as these'.

Jesus did not say we must become childish but child-like with the sincerity and humility of a little child who accepts dependence on others and makes no attempt to hide mistakes.

This surely is the full measure of 'a child of God' - a person who sees them-selves clearly, accepts weaknesses, trusts in God's mercy and love and then, out of love, tries to do what God wants them to do.

Jesus used the parable of the Pharisee and the tax collector to show that we must know ourselves if we are to be truly sincere. The Pharisee went into the temple and thanked God that he was good, that he fasted three times a week and that he gave one-tenth of his income to the church. He saw himself as so much better than the tax collector who stood well back, his head lowered and prayed to God to have pity on him, a sinner.

Jesus used the parable to explain that the tax collector, the sinner, who accepted his faults and asked for forgiveness for them , was greater in God's eyes than the proud Pharisee who could see no fault in himself (Lk 18 : 9-14).

Jose Maria Escriva put this succinctly when he said:

'Don't try to grow up. A child, always a child, even when you are dying of old age. When a child stumbles and falls, no one is surprised, his father promptly lifts him up. When the person who stumbles and falls is older, the immediate reaction is one of surprise and laughter. Sometimes the first impulse passes and the laughter gives way to pity. But older people are expected to get up by themselves...'Be a child; and when you stumble, may you be lifted by the hand of your Father - God'.

Using books and stories for discussion

One of the classic themes of numerous books and stories is the pitfalls facing anyone who lacks sincerity.

Pinocchio, once he comes to life, quickly loses his childlike sincerity and is lured by Stromboli into believing he is a wonderful actor who no longer has any need of his father, Geppetto's, guidance. His lack of sincerity gets him into deeper and deeper trouble as he hides the truth from himself and deceives others.

Fortunately, for Pinocchio he receives a wonderful lesson in sincerity on Pleasure Island. Here all the lost children, who have been deceived into thinking that they could behave as badly as they wished and were responsible to no one for their actions, gradually find themselves turning into donkeys as their insincerity grows. Pinocchio sees the error of his ways in time and eventually turns out to be 'honest, truthful and good' - a truly sincere boy.

Everyday activities we can use to teach sincerity

As parents, we need to encourage children to talk to us especially about themselves. This must become a habit while children are still very young. Teenagers will not suddenly start talking to their parents if they have never done so as children. This basic communication is essential if we, as parents, are to guide our children.

Sincerity is based on children's confidence that their parents love them and want to help them.

To help - not to judge

Children, especially young adolescents, often exaggerate or even lie about their own, or their parents', possessions. On discovering this deception or lie, Mum may admonish children saying how wrong it is to lie. This in itself will do little to help children with the virtue of sincerity. Fear of being humiliated by Mum's scolding may actually persuade children to go to even greater lengths next time to conceal the deception - thus being even less sincere.

However, if Mum sits down with her children and discusses the situation lovingly, pointing out all the non-material things which the children or the family have, an important lesson in sincerity could be given. Mum should try to understand and get the children to understand how the 'peer pressure' may have led them into lying and insincerity. Above all, the children will see the parent as someone who wants to help, not to judge.

Mum will, of course, point out that lying is wrong. But with understanding and love will encourage the children to become more sincere, knowing that Mum wants to help.

Fact or opinion?

Children need to be able to distinguish fact from opinion. Television advertisements often provide parents with the opportunity to help children make this distinction.

Suppose the family is viewing television, when an advertisement for a familiar breakfast cereal appears. It is relatively easy for the parents to point out:

> *What are the facts? ----->'WheatiePops contain vitamins and minerals'*

> *What are the opinions? ----->'Will keep you fit and healthy and help you win sporting trophies'*

As the children become older, more important matters on the television news or in the newspapers can be discussed. This is very important since just about every fact will be presented as opinion and every opinion as fact. Take abortion, for example:

> *What are the facts? - 'The unborn baby is killed'*

> *What are the opinions? - 'It may be in the best interests of the mother'*

Structured examples of sincerity

Really knowing yourself

An interesting exercise here for anyone - parent or child is to draw up a map of a few people who know you best - rating the knowledge that each person has of you. For example, Mum knows me quite well - high rating. My brother hardly knows me at all - low rating.

.

Another interesting and revealing exercise is to list the ten factors that someone needs to know about you before you could give them a perfect score on the above test.

This will serve to help you to examine yourself and paint a picture of the 'real' you.

Perhaps you could divide your list of descriptions into two sections - your pluses and your minuses. What are your best qualities? What are your main weaknesses?

Young adolescents

There is very little need for parents of small children to create structured instances for the purpose of teaching sincerity. Young children who have been encouraged from an early age to be open with their parents, will provide all the opportunities needed to practise this virtue.

However, as children reach the early adolescent years, they are usually less interested in what their parents think and much more concerned with their peers.

It is at this stage that parents need to deliberately find things to discuss with their children - to find opportunities to be involved with their lives.

> *For example, parents should encourage their adolescent children to continue with their sporting activities. The parents should also participate as much as possible in these activities, perhaps by becoming members of the Swimming Club committee or team manager of the child's Soccer Club. In this way, a good line of communication is kept open between the parents and their adolescent children on matters of mutual interest.*

Teenagers should be allowed some privacy without being allowed to shut themselves off from their parents. The dinner time discussion and family prayer time are just as necessary for the unsure teenager as for the formation of the younger child.

If children are confident of parents' love for them they will be encouraged to be sincere. Parents have the duty to guide their children to see themselves as they are - with qualities and abilities but also with weaknesses. They were created this way by God, for a purpose. Whatever their qualities and weaknesses, they are the children of God; loved by parents and loved by God.

Smart Mark talks about orderliness

7. Orderliness

Poor Dad. After all his efforts to instil a bit of order into his children, he is quickly undone by his own lack of orderliness. It is easy to see from this brief glimpse into the life of our family that a lack of orderliness can be a great thief of time.

A few moments spent tidying up our possessions and putting them away in the right place can save us hours of searching and frustration when we next need the object in question.

And, of course, there is little point in preaching orderliness to children if we, as parents, set a bad example of this virtue. In fact it is just about impossible for a child to practise orderliness in an environment which is disorderly.

A common complaint parents have of their children is about the 'mess' they make and their failure to clean up after themselves. As the children get older their capacity to make a mess increases exponentially so that by the time they reach adolescence, the subject of orderliness is often a major cause of conflict between parents and children.

How do families arrive at this state of affairs and what can parents do to instil some sense of orderliness in their children?

To be orderly, we need to organise:

> *1. our possessions*
>
> *2. our time*
>
> *3. the things we do*

Let us look at these three aspects of orderliness.

Organising our possessions

A place for everything and everything in its place

A few years ago, Dad spent some time in a Japanese factory and was amazed to find that the Japanese workers could carry out a task in 20 minutes when workers in the Australian factory took 4 hours to complete the same task!

Expecting to find that the Japanese workers had better equipment, worked harder and took shorter rest breaks, Dad was surprised to find that this was not the case. If anything the Japanese equipment was older and the Japanese workers appeared quite unhurried going about their work compared with their Australian counterparts.

The big difference between the two factories was very simple. In the Japanese factory, all the workers knew exactly what they had to do at any time and all the tools and equipment they needed were neatly stored away in special racks and labelled. The job proceeded smoothly and, when it was finished, everything was put neatly back where it belonged.

On the other hand, in the Australian factory, not everyone was clear as to what they should be doing, people were rushing everywhere, getting in each other's way, nobody could find any of the tools and equipment they wanted and when the job was finished all the workers went for a tea break leaving a mess for someone else to clean up.

Once the Australian factory introduced the same degree of orderliness into their work practices, they soon matched the Japanese 20 minutes for the task in question.

Just like those grown up factory workers, children must be taught from an early age the importance and efficiency of organising their possessions. Before children can be taught to put things away, there must be an orderly system already in operation.

Children cannot possibly put their clothes away in a tidy fashion if the cupboard is in a state of disorder to begin with. However, if there is an area of the cupboard designated for T-shirts, another for shorts and a drawer for socks, then the task is possible and relatively easy.

Organising our time

Life today is fairly hectic. Most families have countless things to do during the day and, it seems, never enough hours to do even half of them. The truth is that most adults are not particularly good at organising their time and as a result give a poor example to their children.

Yet when people find themselves with particular deadlines - getting ready to go away on holiday, for example - and they sit down and make a list of all the things they have to do, lo and behold, as if by magic, they can suddenly get through twice as many jobs as normal with time to spare!

In our family, we find there are three important rules to be followed when organising our time.

Rule 1: Make a list of things to be done within a certain time frame. One of our most vital times of the week is Sunday evening when we sit down with the whole family and simply list the jobs to be completed within the next seven days. It may sound rather basic but without our weekly job's list, life in our family would be completely chaotic.

Rule 2: Discuss the jobs and make sure the priorities are right - that means all of us agreeing which are the most important jobs and not allowing ourselves to be distracted by minor matters.

Rule 3: Avoid the trap of spending too much time doing the things we enjoy rather than the things we really should do. (In our case, this means Dad not spending all day in the garden when the car needs washing and the gutters must be cleaned out. And Mum not spending all day baking cakes when the ironing has not been finished.)

Children are very susceptible to this last problem which prevents them from organising their time.

Organising the things we do

Imagine going on a skiing holiday and arriving at the ski lodge to find that Mum has packed only shorts and T-shirts. The children would be shocked at the mother's lack of organisation and would probably believe she had gone mad.

Of course, this seldom happens because holidays are usually times when people think about and organise what they are doing. But this organisation seems to desert them as soon as they are back into the routine of daily life.

Ironically, it is the people who lead the busiest and most demanding lives who seem to have the least problems fitting everything in. Our Sunday evening planning session sets out the week in detail for each member of the family. Things usually run like clockwork and we are able to pack twice as much into our lives. The only trouble is that we forget to do it sometimes, or on Tuesday we find we have three more jobs than we expected. In these situations, we either panic or pray - usually a bit of both.

How do we teach our children to be orderly?

Talking with the child

Inspiration from scripture and the saints

Jesus preached parables about orderliness. One famous parable from Matthew 24: 36-37 is about the wise and foolish virgins. The wise virgins were models of orderliness - they had prepared their lamps and had enough oil for the possibly long wait for the arrival of the bridegroom. The foolish virgins had not planned ahead well enough for the eventuality that the Bridegroom would arrive late. They had to go out and get more oil, and so missed the wedding celebration - simply because they were not well organised.

Using books and stories for discussion

For younger children, the *Mr Men* books provide many simple discussion topics on the human values. The story of *Mr Messy* and *Mr Tidy* points out even to young children the vice of being disorderly, at both ends of the spectrum, so parents can discuss the virtue of orderliness in a way which is applicable to young children.

Everyday activities we can use to teach orderliness

Like obedience, there are numerous occasions during the day which provide us with the opportunity to teach children orderliness. A few of our favourites are:

• keeping a diary

• sorting and folding the washing into various piles e.g. those that need ironing/those that don't, piles for different members of the family, piles of different types of clothes (socks, pants, etc.)

• keeping a record book of personal information e.g. personal best times at swimming or athletics.

• helping younger brothers and sisters to tidy their toys - always a great favourite as the older brother or sister 'teaches' the younger how to get some order into his/her toys.

• creating a bedtime routine ie. supper - brush teeth - toilet - say prayers - read bedtime story - lights out.

• Getting clothes ready for the next day, the night before, to teach children to think ahead and plan for their different clothes requirements on different days of the week.

Structured examples of orderliness

Regular bed times

Our experience with children is that 'routine' is one of the most valuable allies a parent can have in an orderly household. Of course, routines can be established for all sorts of family activities - from homework to household chores, but one of the most powerful routines is a regular and strictly enforced bedtime for each child.

Of course, a regular bedtime for each child may not be an easy thing to achieve especially when there is a wide age range among the children in the family. But the benefits of a strictly enforced bedtime flow through to many other areas of orderliness which are beneficial to parents and children - homework and household chores must be finished by a certain time if the child is to have time to play before bedtime. Extensions to the normal bedtime can be granted as a treat, say, to watch a special (in the parents' judgment) television program. This will also develop in the child a means of discerning between good quality television and 'junk' which would never be allowed as a reason for missing one's bed time.

School liaison

Most schools, both primary and secondary, have some form of systematic method of liaison with parents. Most common forms of liaison include the homework diary and the weekly newsletter. Parents should take advantage of these 'orderly' means of communication to teach their children the value of orderliness. Homework diaries should be checked regularly. Where a parent's signature or comment is required, the parents should make sure they put some effort into checking and discussing the homework with the child.

Children who learn the value of orderliness while still having only a few tasks to accomplish, will be well prepared for the increased work load as they grow older.

Smart Mark talks about generosity

8. Generosity

It is very difficult to appreciate what constitutes generosity in others. A generous person acts unselfishly and cheerfully for another, knowing one is helping and that it will cost one an effort.

Different forms of generosity

Uncle Jim's $50 cheque would have cost him little effort if he is wealthy - he may well have been simply easing his conscience with this gift, aware that he is far from generous with his time as far as Louise is concerned - he never comes to see the family.

Compared with this token generosity, the afternoon's effort put in by Clare on the home-made birthday card was a very generous act. She gave up much of her time for her sister's benefit and then spent weeks' worth of her pocket money on toffees to stick on the card.

So too with Grandma, who spent much of her pension on the 'bright' wool and lovingly made the jumper to keep her granddaughter warm.

Generosity is not a matter of the material value of what is given - giving material possessions is only one form of giving. There are many other ways in which people, especially children can give. The secret is for parents and children to be aware of what they have which they can give. Their time, energy, work, talents, friendship, forgiveness and even life itself. Children need to be encouraged to give in different ways and not to see generosity as being only about material possessions.

The other side of giving - receiving

In learning to give, children must also learn to receive. This is not always easy in a young child - even a twelve-year-old like Louise surprised Smart Mark by her generosity in receiving her gifts so graciously - even the ones which were not exactly what she would have chosen herself.

For the most part, parents must point out from an early age the true value of things to their children, often by means of the example they set. When a young child works hard to colour a stone found in the garden as a gift for Mum, the way in which Mum accepts the gift will teach the child much about the way to receive. This is not always easy, of course. If Dad is half way through mowing the lawn when his young son wants him to read a story, he has a choice - cheerfully leave the lawn mowing or tactfully suggest that he would enjoy the story better if he could finish the lawn first.

How do we teach our children to be generous

Talking with the child

Inspiration from scripture and the saints:

Many examples of generosity can be found in scripture and the lives of the saints.

The life of Jesus was itself the most generous act although this is a difficult example for young children to relate to. Older children can, however, appreciate that God gave his only Son, Jesus, to die in order to redeem us. Also with older children, the Sermon on the Mount offers good material for a discussion on generosity: 'Love your enemies, do good to those who hate you'. These excerpts from scripture can provide parents with opportunities to discuss real generosity.

If we give just to receive a reward or so that others will think highly of us, in other words for our own benefit, then we are not being truly generous. Similarly, if we are generous only to our friends, this is not true generosity. With younger children, the parable of the Good Samaritan is one which can be used in connection with giving help solely for the benefit of others with no thought for oneself.

The passage from scripture about the widow's mite can be used with young children to point out that it is not the value of the gift which determines the amount of generosity but the act of giving unselfishly relative to the effort on the part of the giver.

The saints provide a multitude of examples of generosity. St Clare was born of rich parents but gave up all she had in order to join the work of St Francis of Assisi - she founded the order of nuns known as the 'Poor Clares'.

St Charles Borromeo also born into a rich Italian family generously gave material possessions to everyone he met, but eventually gave his time, his work, talents and his life to help the poor and sick and to bring people to God.

In our own day we have the example of Mother Teresa who provides an inspiration for us all but especially for young children who can see generosity in this elderly nun working among the poor in Calcutta.

With older children, the story of St Maximilian Kolbe is particularly inspiring. Maximilian gave his life when he took the place of another man marked to die in the Nazi concentration camp of Auschwitz. Sergeant Gajowniczek was married with two children and had been selected to die in the starvation bunker at Auschwitz. Maximilian pointing to the condemned Polish sergeant said 'I would like to take his place because he has a wife and children'.

This is the highest form of generosity - Maximilian gave his life, cheerfully, for the benefit of another because he loved God and his fellow beings.

Fr Damien is another example of saintly generosity. He chose to live and work with the lepers of Molokai. He gave his work, his time, his health and eventually his life when, after sixteen years, he contracted leprosy himself and died.

Using books and stories for discussion

Dickens' great Christmas tale *A Christmas Carol* will always be a favourite with children and can serve to highlight the problems of people who are unable to be generous - as was Ebeneezer Scrooge.

Angelina's Christmas by Katherine Holabird is a great book for young children who will relate to Angelina's generosity towards Old Mr Bill as she visits him regularly with her lemonade gifts.

Structured discussion activities

A task to set children during a car journey:

Use the letters of the word GENEROSITY to write a poem connected with the virtue. This could be an individual effort or done by pairs of children or even a whole family affair, with each person contributing one line.

Another task to set children during a car journey could be to draw a picture (as in Pictionary) which would lead another to guess a particular example of generosity.

Everyday activities we can use to teach generosity

Generosity is connected closely with love for others. We give because we love. It is, therefore, more than any of the human values, to be considered as the 'Family Value.'

By its nature, generosity is acquired by practising many other virtues. There are many naturally occurring situations in any family which you can use to teach generosity. As long as the parents are aware of what they are trying to encourage they will find it easy to use these situations as they arise.

The box of chocolates

A child has been given a box of chocolates or a packet of lollies. The parents may need to direct a young child to offer these to the other children. It is important that the demands of the parents are reasonable. It is not a good idea to encourage the seven-year-old to offer the box of twenty chocolates when there are sixteen guests in the house. His reaction, when he realises that he only has two or three left for himself when the box comes back to him, is likely to be 'If this is generosity, I don't think much of it'. Far better suggest to the young child that he should offer his two best friends a chocolate. He will then see that he can make another person happy with a little effort on his part.

The favourite toy

The above example applies equally to children's favourite toys. Very young children of two or three years old may refuse to part with their favourite toy car. If the parents drag it from them and give it to another child, they will not be helping develop generosity but rather persuade them that generosity is just too hard to handle. In this case it would be a good idea to suggest that they lend the toy car to the other child for five minutes while they play with Mum or Dad with a toy train.

Will you play with me?

Parents cannot always drop everything when children ask them to play with them - nor should they. But, if they are willing regularly to put down the newspaper and switch off the television, to spend some time with the children, they are giving the children a good example of generosity.

When the older children are asked to play with their younger brothers and sisters, they have a great opportunity to be generous. Parents need to be aware of these situations so that they can help with advice or guidance when needed.

For example, twelve-year-old Louise has just finished her homework in time to watch a television program she enjoys, when seven-year-old Clare asks 'Will you play Lego with me'. Louise has a choice of responses to Clare:

1. No, I want to watch my favourite program.

2. Yes, but after this program is finished.

3. All right, I'll play now and watch a different program later.

Regular answers like (1) point to a lack of generosity on Louise's part which would need to be tackled by her parents. One way to point out this lack of generosity to Louise would be for Mum or Dad to play with Clare for a while and leave dinner until later. Parents would then have to point out clearly to Louise that she is being selfish in her attitude. Even (2) type answers which are acceptable at times must not become a regular answer or there is a danger that Louise will develop a weak response to generosity - I will be generous but only when it suits me.

Generosity involves making an effort for the benefit of another. This will involve giving our time even when *it is not convenient for us.*

Receiving generously

Many opportunities will arise when we can guide our children to receive generously.

Children should be encouraged to say thank-you for every gift they receive. If the gift is from an aunt or uncle who lives interstate or overseas, a letter or telephone call will be required.

When young children receive a present they don't like, they may need to be guided in receiving. A parent will need to explain that the gift was given as a sign of love. Older children are more likely to appreciate this fact and they should give a good example to their younger brothers and sisters of how to receive graciously. As early as possible young children should be made to see the gift as coming from someone who loves them rather than simply to see the gift as an object with only intrinsic value - the pink and yellow jumper knitted for Louise by Grandma was a most generous gift even though, for Louise, it had no intrinsic value.

Receiving invitations and time given

Parents themselves must be aware of the example they give their children in receiving invitations or time given to them by others - perhaps in the form of a visit from a friend or an offer by a child to read them a story.

If the children hear parents commenting that they have been invited to dinner by Mrs Jones but they will find some excuse to refuse the invitation, this is a bad example for children in the art of receiving.

Similarly, the parent who is always too busy to receive the time young children want to give them to read a story, is telling the children that receiving is only important when it is convenient.

As parents, we must be aware that there are many opportunities in the day to receive - whenever possible, we must receive generously.

When the seven -year-old offers to wash up, accept the offer even if it means you may have to wash the glasses and precious dishes again later. Take the gift and receive it as generously as it is offered.

When an older child offers to help a younger one with homework or piano practice, praise both the giving and receiving as acts of generosity.

Structured examples of generosity

Birthday and Christmas gifts

This structured activity lends itself to the investigation of two important factors in connection with the human value of generosity:

1. what do I have that I can give?

2. how can I best benefit the other person?

Helping seven-year-old Clare with the value of generosity

1. What has she to give?

A few weeks before Christmas, Mum discusses with Clare the problem of Christmas presents for her brothers and sisters. Clare is guided by her parents to consider what she has that she can give. Her time - she can spend time making them things. Her talents - she can write well for her age, she can draw, sing and has a few origami skills. But she cannot knit or do cross-stitch as well as her twelve-year-old sister can.

She has a little money but not really enough to buy much with and she has a few bits and pieces among her possessions which could be used.

2. How can she benefit others?

Considering what she has to give, how can this be best used to provide a Christmas gift for her baby brother Mark, her twelve-year-old sister Louise and her eighteen-year-old brother David?

The baby first - he will play with any new toy which is bright and noisy. Among her own bits and pieces, Clare has a collection of old cotton reels. She will paint them in bright colours and thread them on a string. Mum offers to find a piece of strong cord to tie up the reels and Clare sets to work to do the rest. As she works, Clare comes up with the really good idea of putting the letters of Mark's name on the four red reels in the middle - so that Mark can learn his name as he plays.

Louise is quite easy to please. She is very keen on athletics and also spends a fair bit of her money on stationery. With Mum's help, Clare decides to buy an exercise book for fifty cents and a packet of special athletics stickers. Mum helps Clare to cover the exercise book in contact and stick the athletics stickers and a picture of Louise's favourite athlete - Debbie Flintoff-King onto the front cover. Clare uses the computer to print a title for the book in a decorative style - 'Athletics Records Book - Louise'. The result is a very special book in which Louise can record her achievement times in her favourite sport.

Clare is so pleased with this idea that she suggests that she does the same for her brother David, but this time related to his favourite sport - swimming. But, with Mum's guidance Clare realises that David is no longer interested in competitive swimming and keeping records of his achievement times, so he would probably not use the book. Clare comes up with a range of ideas; she is really keen to make a tape for him on which she sings some of her favourite songs. She would enjoy that - but would David? Probably not - but Mum tactfully suggests that this would be an even better idea for Dad who would really treasure a tape of his daughter singing, to play in the car. Eventually, they come up with the idea of a jar decorated with coloured ribbon containing some lollies and a card for David in which Clare offers to make his bed for a week - an act of true generosity and seven days of that is long enough for a seven-year-old!

Generosity outside the family

There are many people in need both in our own community and in the rest of the world. Most parents will find it easy to target a group for attention - it may be the St Vincent de Paul group who provide for the needy, a particular mission charity known to the parents or linked with the child's school, or The Royal Childrens Hospital - with a set appeal day on Good Friday.

Let's say, for example, that we wish to encourage seven -year-old Clare and twelve-year-old Louise to exercise generosity with regard to missionary countries. At Clare's school, a mission has been adopted which helps old people in Sri Lanka. For one week during Lent the children and their families make a special sacrifice, - going without desserts after dinner or soft drinks with lunch. On the final Friday of Lent the school lunch is sacrificed and all children at the school buy a bread roll. Parents could help the children to calculate how much money has been saved by their sacrifices during the week and this amount is sent to the mission.

There are many other structured activities similar to this example, run by various organisations, which can be used equally well by parents to teach their children the virtue of generosity. These would include the World Vision 40-Hour Famine held in June each year in which people are sponsored to fast for forty hours and donate the proceeds to overseas aid. Older children can participate fully in the 40-Hour Famine, younger ones can be encouraged to replace one or two meals with light snacks. This active participation in works of charity such as these also involves children in the practice of other virtues such as fortitude, particularly when a sacrifice over a long period is needed (forty hours is a very long time for a twelve-year-old). The World Vision sponsorship program can provide parents with another example to use to teach generosity. In this program, Australian families adopt children in developing countries and support them financially.

Teenagers and older children may be encouraged to give part of their pocket money or job earnings to a child sponsorship. This commitment would involve more than generosity - the commitment would be long term; hence, children would also be practising responsibility, respect for others and, of course, the theological virtue of charity.

Another means of being generous outside the family is the St. Vincent de Paul poor man's Mass which collects food, goods and money for needy people.

Giving our time

Parents could arrange, after discussion with their children, for them to visit an elderly neighbour, Grandma or a friend in hospital. Sometimes this may arise from the visits made by parents to these people.

Visiting Mr Wilson: Mum takes Mr Wilson shopping every Thursday. Mr Wilson is in his early 80's and his needs are few - he enjoys his short visit to the shops and he enjoys the company and cup of coffee when the shopping is finished.

Louise decides Mr Wilson would like a visit from her, perhaps on a regular weekly basis. (She may be led to this decision by Mum's suggestion). Each Saturday, following Little Athletics, Louise calls in to see Mr Wilson, who lives close to the athletics track. She has a cup of tea, tells him about her morning at the athletics and reads bits of the newspaper to him as poor eyesight makes reading difficult for him. Both Louise and Mr Wilson look forward to the visits and Louise sometimes has to arrange her time in a way which is inconvenient for her. But, she learns to appreciate that effort is needed in order to spend the time which means so much to Mr Wilson.

Children, and parents for that matter, can learn much from elderly grandparents. Even substitute grandparents have much to offer children in their growing years. Parents should make every effort to visit grandparents regularly. If they live too far away, regular letters should become a habit for the children. In this modern age, children can even be encouraged to make videos to send to grandparents who live interstate or overseas. In all of these ways, they are learning to give their time generously to benefit others.

One thing that cannot be stressed too much is the importance of parental example with regard to generosity. Generosity is a value closely connected with love. We give because we love. It is therefore a vital family value and there are literally hundreds of occasions which arise naturally in the course of a week which parents can use to guide their children in the practice of generosity.

Smart Mark talks about industriousness

9. Industriousness

Before parents can teach the human value of industriousness, they must be clear as to what this value is. To be industrious, a person needs to:

1. do some work which requires disciplined effort

2. be diligent in this work.

Let us look at these two aspects of industriousness.

Work requires disciplined effort

In order to be able to practise industriousness, it is essential to have some work which requires hard, disciplined effort and is appropriate to the age and ability of the person. For Dad, it may be the professional job at the office. For Mum, it may be cleaning, cooking and taking care of baby. For school-aged children, it could mean putting effort into school studies. For older children this may be extended to include the work needed to put effort into sport or become more proficient at a musical instrument.

A small child will not differentiate between work and play - they consider all play to be work, and all work to be play.

When is work - work?

It is important to realise that work may not only be the particular 'job' which one does. Dad's work may be looking after the garden, bathing the children, helping a child with piano practice or, if he has time left, improving his own tennis serve.

Mum may work outside the home in a professional capacity. She may work in the home making curtains, washing clothes or cooking meals. She may work to learn another language or her work may involve writing letters to friends and relatives abroad.

Children's work too can take many forms. The only requirement is that it needs effort and discipline and is appropriate to the age and ability of the child.

Appropriateness of the work

In order to practise industriousness, it is important that the work is appropriate to the age and ability of the child. It is also important to distinguish between the effort put into the work and the quality of the completed task - they are not the same.

It is impossible to develop this value if we ask a five-year-old to write a critique on the work of St Thomas Aquinas. Regardless of the amount of effort the child puts into this task, he is not capable of producing a good piece of work.

Conversely, if we ask a twelve-year-old to complete half a dozen simple sums such as $3 + 4 = ?$, in an hour, we are not asking them to put any effort at all into this task. Completing this work to perfection, gives the child no practice in industriousness.

If Mum supplies an evening meal of beans on toast for the family, she is not practising industriousness - the task is too easy for her. But, the same task given to a six-year-old may be a very good opportunity for the child to carefully consider what is needed and industriously set about this challenging task.

Diligence in work

The human value of industriousness not only requires a person to work hard but also to work diligently. Diligence comes from the Latin word *diligo* which means 'to love and choose after careful consideration'.

Therefore, to be diligent, we must do our work lovingly and thoughtfully. Doing a job well is an act of love. Children may work lovingly because their parents have asked them to and they want to show their parents that they love them.

We may work diligently (lovingly) because we want to thank God for the talents he has given us. God made each of us his 'special' children. If we put something of ourselves into our work, we are doing what he wants us to do.

Let us remember St Joseph who gave us the most glorious example of work when he cared for the child Jesus and His Mother Mary. How lovingly he applied himself to his daily work. No wonder St Joseph has earned himself the title of Patron Saint of Workers.

How do we teach our children to be industrious?

Talking with the child

Inspiration from scripture and the saints

The example of St Joseph, as quoted above, is an appropriate way to begin discussing the meaning of industriousness with children. This humble saint is an excellent example of one who did have hard, disciplined work to do and did it diligently. Consider, with the children, the birth of Jesus in Bethlehem, the flight into Egypt and the years of work Joseph gave to bringing up the Child Jesus and caring for his Mother Mary.

Many other saints provide inspirational examples of industriousness. St John Bosco, although experiencing great difficulties with his studies for the priesthood, continued his work diligently and was in fact ordained at the age of twenty-six; so enabling him to continue to work to save poor boys from starvation and moral danger.

From scripture, many examples provide a starting point for discussing industriousness. The parable of the Talents is one obvious example - in which the child can be taught that the work they do is one way of thanking God for the gifts they have been given.

The fact that Jesus himself spent thirty years doing ordinary work and only three years in public life, is another discussion point for parents pointing to the importance of work in everyone's life.

The episode related in Luke's Gospel (Lk 10: 38-41), where Jesus speaks to Martha and Mary, is yet another example which could be used to discuss industriousness. This would be especially relevant with older children in pointing to the danger of knowing when to rest and why to rest.

Rest, meditation, holidays and sleep are important to all of us if we are to be well equipped to work diligently - they are essentials not luxuries.

Children can be encouraged to pray regularly for industriousness in themselves and others:

to say a 'state of life' prayer' in which they call on God to direct them to the work appropriate to them as they grow into adult maturity;

to appreciate the importance of the morning offering in which they offer their daily work to God.

This will ensure that any work they do diligently will be a means of grace. The work may be unseen by others; it may be thought of by others as being of little importance; but if it is done thoughtfully and lovingly and offered to God, the rewards reaped from this work will be great.

Using books and stories for discussion

The book *The Agony and the Ecstasy* by Irving Stone tells the story of the industriousness of the famous artist Michelangelo. Michelangelo worked diligently on his artistic ventures. *The Agony and the Ecstasy* is useful for teenage children. It shows not only industriousness, as practised by Michelangelo in his great sculptures and his work on the Sistine Chapel, but also points out the vice of being too industrious so that the work becomes all consuming.

For younger children, the *Mr Men* books provide many simple discussion points on the virtues. The story of *Mr Lazy* points out even to young children the vice of laziness so parents can discuss industriousness in a way which is applicable to young children.

Using structured discussion activities

Flowers at the dinner table

Make some paper flowers, one for each member of the family on which are written the following questions:

• *What job do you want to do when you grow up?*

• *What is the hardest work you have had to do in your life?*

• *Who is the hardest worker you know? (or similar)*

During the course of the meal, each member of the family picks one flower, reads the question and answers it as best they can. Then it is open for the other family members to answer or add comments of their own. This may be too structured for some families; for others it may be very rewarding.

This game can also be adapted easily for the car - using a dice and a set of cards with questions on them - or for other human values as selected by the parents.

Everyday activities to teach industriousness

Completing homework assignment

This example will probably apply to every child from about the age of eight years and it provides a good opportunity for parents to help the child practise industriousness.

Stages involved

Encourage the child to write down what is asked of them by teachers as the message often gets distorted in passage between school and home and nothing is worse than working diligently on the wrong assignment.

1. Clarify the work to be done

- What is the task exactly?
- When is it to be done?
- What do you need in order to do the work?
  (Pens, paper, research materials, notes)
- How long do you estimate it will take?
- How will you begin, continue, end?

Some of this will arise from clarifying the work to be done but it is wise to go over the points again.

2. What is required before the task is done well?

- What information will you need to include?
- How will you edit it?
- Will you do a rough draft?
- How will you cope with mistakes?
- Will Mum or Dad check it?
- How will you present it?

3. How will you motivate the child to work diligently?

- Why are you doing this - will it help you directly or indirectly?
- Will the teacher look at it/mark it?
- Can you put as much of yourself as possible into this work so that you can offer it as a gift to God for the talents he has given you?

Preparing tea

This activity can become a regular daily way to help children of all ages to practise industriousness.

Stages Involved

1. Clarify the Work to be Done

The child setting the table may need to consider:

- Which table cloth will I use - where is it?
- How many places will I set?
- What cutlery is needed - do we need soup spoons tonight?

Each child will have their own set tasks to do - the youngest lays out the placemats and cutlery - another may dish out the vegetables - another to prepare and say grace before meals.

Each child must be sure of exactly what is required. Initially this may take some time, hence it is a good idea to have any particular job for at least a week, so that the child becomes familiar with the requirements.

2. What is required before the task is done well?

- Is the table cloth straight?
- Are the placemats neat and tidy?
- Is the cutlery in the correct position?

3. How will you motivate the child to work diligently?

This is not so easy with commonplace jobs. It may be necessary to make a special comment on jobs well done - a smile may be enough - a note made of the attempt of a child to be original (names on the place-mats, flowers on the table).

Getting ready for school

This can be adapted for getting ready to stay overnight at a friend's house, a week's holiday at the beach or for a visit to Grandma's.

Stages Involved

Each child in the family can have a particular responsibility but in this case each child will also have to get themselves ready to some extent, depending on the age and ability of the child.

Much of the preparation for school needs to take place prior to the morning itself and is closely related to the human value orderliness.

---

1. Clarify the work to be done

- Are your clothes clean and ready and your shoes polished?
- What do you need to take?
- When will you pack your things?
- When will you get up - have a wash - have breakfast - leave the house?

---

2. What is required before the task is done well?

- Did you make good preparations the night before school?
- Did you get up in good time?
- How well did you tackle unforeseen circumstances?
- Were you rushed or in full control?

This routine job can be done well if children put something of themselves into it and are well organised.

---

3. How will you motivate the child to work diligently?

This is a difficult one unless the child is orderly. Positive feedback from Mum and Dad on a job well done is one of the best ways to motivate a child. Don't forget the importance of the example of industriousness and orderliness early in the morning given by parents themselves.

Structured examples to teach industriousness

Writing a letter

This activity is applicable to all children from about the age of three or four years. Little children can get Mum and Dad to write and then the children draw the pictures. There are many reasons for writing a letter: 1) to thank someone for a gift, 2) at Christmas or for someone's birthday, 3) for a relative you don't see very often.

Stages involved

Parents can provide an example to copy from and can discuss with the children

1. Clarify the work to be done

- What type of letter is it to be:
- Why are we writing?
- To whom are we writing?
- What is the format of the letter?
- What can I write about?
- How long should the letter be?

2. What is required before the task is done well?

- Will you prepare a rough draft or notes first?
- How will you check your spelling?
- What will you do about mistakes?

3. How will you motivate the child to work diligently?

- Is there a point to this letter? (make sure there is)
- Can this be the best letter you have ever written
- How -why (discuss with the child)
- Will it bring happiness to someone?

Planting a garden

Stages involved

1. **Clarify the work to be done**

   - Where will your patch be? (mark it out)
   - What will you plant?
   - How and when will you carry out the initial planting?
   - How will you maintain the garden?

2. **What is required before the task is done well?**

   - What equipment will you need?
   - What preparations are needed to prepare soil/protect plants?
   - How will you clean up afterwards?

3. **How will you motivate the child to work diligently?**

   - What is the garden for?
     (grow flowers to give to others, herbs to sell at school fete, vegetables for family meals)

Make sure that the work matches the age of the child. If this is to be a family concern, the four-year-old may be allocated a two-metre border strip for flowers, the seven-year-old a vegetable patch and the teenager a separate herb garden.

A list may be needed of on-going commitments and even a time arranged for these duties. This also involves orderliness.

Motivation is not difficult in the case of a garden because all children love to see the wonder of new life and growth.

Making presents

This is a good structured activity which needs a little preparation on the part of parents to come up with a suitable person for whom the present can be made and a relevant gift depending on the age and ability of the child.

Stages involved

> With young children it is essential to have the ideas clearly in your mind before you start. Older children's ideas of what they may make for Aunt Joan may also need some modification. Allow plenty of time before the occasion.

1. Clarify the work to be done

- For whom is the present ?
- What is the occasion?
- What would she like that you can make?
  (point in discussing a patchwork quilt with a six year-old)
- What do I need to have and do to make it?

2. What is required before the task is done well?
If Louise has decided to make a cross-stitch for Aunt Joan, she may consider:
- Is the finished work free from mistakes?
- Is it nicely framed?
- Are the colours well matched?
- Is the picture about cats? (Aunt Joan loves cats)

3. How will you motivate the child to work diligently?
Why not just buy her something instead?
- She will appreciate this special gift - there won't be another like it.
- I will have used my talents to show my love for God and provide happiness to my special aunt.
- I'll never find anything as appropriate as this at the shops.

Industriousness, once established, is self-perpetuating as even a young child can gain immense satisfaction from a job well done. It will be obvious in many of these examples that orderliness is often connected with the virtue of industriousness.

Conclusion

There is a great overlap from one human value to another. They have been presented here, for clarity, under separate headings but the good news for parents is that, in teaching one value, we actually teach many others also.

The other good news is that we learn from our teaching. In helping our children to acquire human values, we will automatically develop these in ourselves.

The outline given here is presented as a practical guide for parents to help their children acquire human values. We hope these practical examples will be beneficial but we must acknowledge that the most important help any parent can give their children is to pray for them. This practical guide can never take the place of prayer. Prayer must be our first responsibility as parents.

*Dear Lord, we implore you
to take our children into your care
and enclose them in the love of your Sacred Heart.
Mary and Joseph, dear parents of the Child Jesus,
intercede for us
that we may bring up our children in the love of God
and one day attain, with them,
the eternal happiness of heaven.*